What Others Are Saying

Jayne Mattson's newest book—*You, You, Me, You*—is a fantastic read for anyone looking to build his/her reputation and career in today's fast-changing and competitive marketplace.

Networking continues to be a critical skill for individuals in transition and independent business owners who are looking around the corner for their next opportunity. Jayne's methodology is a great way to make positive success in what might be a challenging exercise for many.

> Ed Evarts, Leadership Coach, Strategist, and Author of *Raise Your Visibility & Value: Unlock the Lost Art of Connecting on the Job*

By honing in on the human connection and the power of genuine conversation, Jayne M. Mattson motivates readers to focus on others first. In *You, You, Me, You*, Mattson offers action steps to help you see that "everyone, including yourself, has something to offer." The goal of networking either to land a job, or to make a new friend is giving something, not getting something, she writes. Mattson's honest, straightforward advice provides the tools we all need to create long-lasting relationships that bring meaning to our lives.

> Kerry Hannon, *New York Times*, *PBS Next Avenue*, AARP columnist and author of *Great Jobs for Everyone 50+* and *Love Your Job*

You, You, Me, You is a much-needed guide to help readers navigate the fine art of building and sustaining relationships. Dale Carnegie would be proud. Jayne refers to the first 9 Principles from *How to Win Friends and Influence People.* Becoming genuinely interested in others, listening, smiling, and talking in terms of other's interests are just a few of the leadership principles from Dale Carnegie's book relating to becoming a friendlier person Jayne effectively weaves throughout her book.

Carolyn Raitt, ELI-MP, SHRM-SCP,
Dale Carnegie Trainer

"Jayne is an accomplished facilitator, trainer and coach. She inspires individuals to explore areas in their lives that block them from achieving their highest potential and helps them develop confidence building skills." This short description was taken from her biography the last time that she presented at the Women's Summit at Bryant University in 2016.

I am the Co-Founder and Director of the Women's Summit at Bryant University in Smithfield, RI. I have worked on this conference for the past 23 years and have encountered hundreds of speakers over the years. Jayne is an outstanding speaker and has presented at the Women's Summit on six different occasions either with a co presenter or by herself.

Jayne has presented at the Women's Summit in 2009, 2010, 2011, 2012, 2013, 2014, and 2016 for a total of seven breakout session in 8 years! Jayne's evaluations of her presentations either in conjunction with her friend or by herself were always excellent.

In Jayne's evaluation in 2016 her ratings were 100% in the good to excellent range in her "Knowledge of Subject", "Effectiveness of Communication", and "Content". Additional comments were, "Please have her come back!" "Jayne was absolutely motivating and wonderful." "I enjoyed that the session was interactive and provided me with things that I can work on to improve myself." "Excellent" "Energetic and informative, very dynamic. Reads the audience well and responds to the scenarios well." "Wonderful speaker, very interactive session." "Great job."

These comments were right off of her evaluation sheet. You cannot make up comments like this! They speak to her comfort and ease of presenting and knowledge of her subject.

On a personal level, Jayne has a very warm and open personality. She is positive, cheerful, and follows up through the years to remain connected.

I would endorse Jayne for any speaking engagement or any professional opportunity that she is seeking.

You will be most fortunate to have Jayne working with you on any project or conference.

Kati Machtley, Director, Bryant University's
"The Women's Summit"

Jayne has led several seminars for young professionals through her support of the Boston Young Professionals Association, and has helped so many of our members advance their careers; from those striving to succeed at their first "real" job, to those looking to move into the next stages of their career.

While there are several details that set Jayne apart, one item that I have always noticed and appreciated is how Jayne greets many attendees at the door, introducing herself and asking each person a little about them. In contrast to a speaker that hoovers around the stage during arrivals, Jayne uses her energy to set the tone for the seminar and attendees make their next steps into the room fully engaged in the session that is about to begin. This practice, along with Jayne's energy and how genuine she is in supporting early to mid career professionals causes attendees to be both relaxed and excited—they know they've come to a great workshop, and aren't shy about participating when the time comes.

Jayne leads by example, in two, but equally important ways. During her workshops, she both teaches techniques and facilitates attendees as they practice them. As she moves about the room, her energy is still just as contagious. With the multiple sessions Jayne has partnered with BostonYPA on, I've never seen someone slump down or participate less than 100%. People actually put their phones away. Jayne also practice what she preaches, which is equally important. I remember listening during her first session and smiling to myself because I could predict how she would follow up—not only was I correct, but Jayne is believable when she speaks and that inspires attendees to get started and follow her advice.

Jayne is wonderful at developing relationships with young professionals and understanding their unique position and challenges. We're grateful for the individual support she's given our members and are always looking forward to planning the next workshop.

Erica Mellone, President, BostonYPA (Boston Young Professional Organization)

Jayne defines the essence of networking perfectly and supports the definition with practical examples that will help US build relationships first. *You, You, Me, You* equates to a powerful use of 14,000 words. I can't wait to share this book with my friends, colleagues and clients.

Mark Lockett, Vice President Corporate Leadership Development and Training, Verastem Oncology

YOU, YOU, ME, YOU

The Art of Talking to People, Networking and Building Relationships

JAYNE MATTSON

Dedication

To my husband, Raphael August Mattson (aka, my Honey Bunch), who has supported me in everything I've done in my professional and personal life. Truth be told, there were times when he wanted success a little more for me than I wanted it for myself. Raphael's support and encouragement from "I want to write a book" to "I wrote a book!" was my guiding light.

To my father, Alfred (Al) Raymond Matthews, who was a major influencer in my life and led me to write about building relationships. Giving me Dale Carnegie's book *How to Win Friends and Influence People* when I was fifteen was a pivotal moment in my life. While writing this book I felt my father's presence in every word and chapter along the way.

To these two very important men in my life, and Dale Carnegie too, I say THANK YOU!

Contents

Foreword

We all know that to achieve our goals in life we have to put ourselves out there and jumpstart relationships with strangers. Career success requires networking and the willingness to join different organizations and move to new cities. We work with unfamiliar people with every re-organization and merger, and every time we travel to meet new customers and business partners. Outside of work, being successful and happy often means joining new schools, new clubs and new organizations, or starting new hobbies. Each of these lead to more interactions with the unfamiliar. *Ultimately, our success is built on how well we can make positive first impressions and expand our network of relationships.*

Unfortunately, developing relationships is not something we learn in school, and our digital world gives us little practice in having real conversations. Still, we've all had thousands of introductions and interactions with new people—so why aren't we confident masters at it by now?

More specifically, how do we ensure we make a positive first impression and develop the relationships we need to be successful and happy? How do we overcome the natural reluctance and nervousness that comes with meeting new people? How do we nurture those relationships the second, third, and 1000th time we meet? How do we avoid talking too much and boring the other person, or talking too little and not getting what we want out of the conversation?

I first met Jayne Mattson back in 2016 soon after I had published my book "What to Do When You're New." We shared a common interest in helping people network and build relationships. When she described her concept of "You, You, Me, You," I was amazed at both the simplicity and power of this conversational technique. So much so that I wrote about her success formula in a *Psychology Today* blog.

I am thrilled that Jayne has published this book and made her unique approach available to everyone.

There are lots of books and techniques out there on how to mingle, make conversation and get to know people, but often the advice not something you can really apply in the heat of the moment when you're starting a conversation. "You, You, Me, You" is easy to remember and remind yourself about as you interact with others. And by recognizing and avoiding the less effective alternatives—for example, a "Me, Me, Me, You" or a "You, You, You, You" conversation—you can ensure that the other person walks away energized and open to another interaction.

In this book Jayne also helps you learn how to deal with conversation challenges such as Self-Absorbed Suzies, Needy Neds and Pushy Petes. Practice the ideas in this book and I know you will quickly see results and enter into new conversations with more confidence and comfort.

Don't let your awkwardness or anxiety with networking and new relationships stop you from getting what you want out of life. *You, You, Me, You* can make a difference.

Keith Rollag, Ph.D.
Dean, F.W. Olin Graduate School of Business,
Babson College
Author of *What To Do When You're New: How to Be Confident, Comfortable and Successful in New Situations*"

Preface

I am passionate about helping people understand what networking really is and how it is done effectively. I've read many articles on how to network, best practices, the dos and don'ts and the many different approaches people use. Each author did a nice job defining networking with the common theme being "networking is about building relationships." However, I noticed that something was dramatically missing from each article. There was an assumption that people knew **how to build relationships**.

If you don't know how to build and maintain relationships, then how can you possibly network effectively? With so much focus on social media and technology, I became very concerned we were going to lose the importance of the face- to-face aspect of relationship building. I didn't want people to lose the human connection to each other. Then, I had the "ah ha" moment! I will write *a book on how to build and sustain relationships using my concept of four simple words.*

*Relationship building is about "**YOU, YOU, ME, YOU**"!*

> "You can make more friends in two months by becoming interested in other people than you can in two years getting people interested in you."
>
> —Dale Carnegie

Jayne Mattson©

CHAPTER ONE

Where It All Began

Relationships have absolutely been the key to my success in my professional and personal life. When I was in my mid-teens, my father gave me a book he bought at a flea market: a 1945 48th Edition of Dale Carnegie's well-known, *How to Win Friends and Influence People*. The book's edges were tattered, the discolored beige pages were worn, and the original owner's name was scrawled across the inside cover.

My father told me, "Honey, honey, honey, if you read this book, you will always be successful." There were always three honeys.

I thought the world of my father, so if he said I would be successful if I read this book, then I was going to read it. And I did, again and again. Every single year I read the book, putting into practice many of the principles Dale Carnegie advocated. Little did I know that a tattered book from a flea market would become the book that influenced my life and prompted me to write my own book about relationships.

My father was a very successful man, probably more than many. It was not because he made a lot of money. The opposite was true. My father, Alfred R. Matthews, was an entrepreneur before people even knew what that meant. To share a few of his endeavors, he bought 2,000 left-footed sneakers because he was going to sell the rubber; then there were the 300 big bowling balls with no holes (not quite sure how someone was intending to bowl); and he imported tiki logs from Hawaii. I can't quite remember what happened with all these deals, but he always had an idea and potential use for them. I remember asking him, "Why are you doing all of this?" His reply was "I want to leave something for you kids."

I could write an entire book about my father and what he tried to do in his life for his family. Maybe he was not a successful businessman leaving his children money, but he gave us so much more. What he did leave us were memories of a man who loved us unconditionally and the legacy of being regarded by so many people as a wonderful human being.

My dad loved life and people and treated everyone he met as if they were the most special person in the room. By profession, my father was a salesman who had his own business when we were growing up, then worked for a company as he got older. As I continued reading Dale Carnegie's book, I began to realize that my father was a version of Dale himself. He practiced so many of the principles that, I too began to apply Dale's principles.

To be successful does not always mean making money. For my father, it was about developing and maintaining relationships with everyone he met. He was active in the community, participating in charity work and he was a licensed auctioneer who helped the city dispose of unclaimed materials and equipment. He had a wonderful sense of humor and worked a crowd like no one else. Everyone loved him.

When my father died, the flag in our hometown was flown at half-mast to honor his contribution to the community. The day of the funeral, as we drove through the city, I felt such deep love and pride. I was honored to have a father who was so respected and beloved by his town.

I was blessed to receive this lesson so early in life that being successful was not about things. Success was about the people you meet, how you treat them, how they treat you, what they say about you when you are not in the room and how you make them feel.

This book is to simplify the lessons from Dale Carnegie and my father for you to improve your relationships. I developed a simple concept on how to build relationships. In this time of social media and technology, this concept can help you be the next Dale Carnegie, or even better, Alfred R. Matthews!

So, let's begin!

CHAPTER TWO

Know Yourself

It may sound crazy, but the skill of being comfortable talking to another human is becoming a lost art. Growing up with my father's influence and the impact of Dale Carnegie in my life, I can't let that happen! This book will help you talk to people, network, and build relationships in today's world.

Before we dive into the process of *You, You, Me, You* and building relationships, let me ask you a very personal question about your core beliefs regarding people and the human spirit: Would you say you love, like, or tolerate people?

How you answer that question has deep significance. If you don't always see the value of meeting new people, being curious about what they do or that everyone has something to offer, you might want to assess your beliefs and how they originated.

Our inner beliefs determine how we live our lives. We often hold onto beliefs from childhood and sometimes do not question their validity as an adult. Many times, we do not even realize we have embedded beliefs. We all do.

Our beliefs affect our ability to build healthy personal and professional relationships. Therefore, if your core beliefs about people are not positive, and you focus on the negatives of what people say, you might struggle with building and maintaining relationships. You might unknowingly look at people and building relationships as a transaction and not as an emotional connection.

Earlier, I told you about my father's ability to build relationships with people, which inspired me to be like him. That was a gift that has value beyond measure. He gave me another gift, perhaps worth even more. He instilled confidence within me as far back as I can remember. If there was something I wanted to achieve, he would say "Honey, honey, honey, of course you can do it."

When I was in my 20's, I wanted to be on the board of our company's credit union, running for the Secretary role. When I told my father, he said, "Why aren't you running for President?"

He saw beyond what I thought I wanted and instilled in me that there was nothing I couldn't do. If I tried and didn't succeed, I focused on what I learned and moved on without beating myself up. To this day, I take on challenges, like writing this book, with very little self-doubt.

However, my life was not all sunshine and roses. When I was thirteen years old, my mother passed away suddenly. She was just forty-four. My father was left with six children to raise, ages five to eighteen. After her death, I struggled with a low self-image that held me back in certain areas. When my negative beliefs started to affect my confidence and relationships, I worked on understanding the "why" and changed my inner negative beliefs to positive ones.

A quote that has always resonated with me is "We are not responsible for what happens to us as children, but we are responsible for what happens to us as adults."

Once you understand what beliefs get in your way, you can begin to replace the negative ones of the past with more positive messages of the present. Your relationships with others will improve, you will become a much happier person, and you will reflect a more positive image for others to see. The most important relationship you have is the one with yourself.

First you must know yourself. Give some thought to these questions:

- When you meet someone, do you remember something positive about them? Or do you focus on something negative?
- Do you find yourself becoming impatient or easily annoyed with others who are not like you?
- Do you believe everyone has something to offer, to contribute to the world? Your world too?

These questions are an initial gauge for you to begin to self-reflect on how you see people.

Even if you find that you lean a little towards the negative, you can shift your perspective. The more you realize that everyone, including yourself, has something to offer, the easier it becomes to connect with others.

When I entered the field of Career Management, some of the keys to my success were my willingness to ask for help, being comfortable meeting new people, and being interested and curious in what others were doing. As a result of my focusing on others first, everyone I met wanted to help me in my career.

One of my colleagues, Ed, once said to me, "Jayne, you have the ability to quickly draw people into meaningful conversations." When I hosted my young nieces and nephews for sleepovers with Auntie Jayne, they were well prepared that, along with pizza, junk food and fun, there would be thought-provoking questions. I asked them various queries, such as: "What is the best thing you like about yourself? If there was one thing you would want to change, what would it be? How would your friends describe you?" One of my godchildren Ashley used to say, "Being with Auntie Jayne is like taking an essay test."

When I am with my group of women friends, there are also questions that I like to ask: *Who had the greatest influence on your life and why? What have you learned about yourself over the past year? Do you have any regrets in your life and if so, what are they?* I have always been interested and curious about other people. I have found that by asking questions, it draws out others to talk more about themselves. Dale Carnegie's advice has proven true. I have made plenty of friends by becoming interested in them instead of trying to get people interested in me. And it has absolutely helped my career.

CHAPTER THREE

You, You, Me, You

In my work as a Career Management Consultant, I have helped people in all phases of their careers. One of the most important aspects of my coaching and consulting is helping clients gain confidence in their abilities and in themselves. One essential skill for job search and career success is knowing how to effectively network.

To gain an understanding of a client's comfort level regarding networking, I often ask, "Are you comfortable meeting new people and asking for help? Do you know how to network effectively?" The responses would vary: "Depends what I am asking." "Sometimes." and "I think I know how to network."

Throughout my conversations and trainings with clients, I pay close attention to what they share during their networking meetings. Mostly, I hear about what they *wanted from* others. Rarely did I hear what they *learned about* others. Things were very lopsided.

It became evident to me that my client's skill set of relationship building outside their work environment was lacking. Many knew how to build relationships *within* their company partly because there were norms and behaviors people followed that supported the culture. However, when they *left* the company, their relationship skills seemed to fall apart.

Clients were entering a new networking situation with the goal of getting something, not thinking of giving. They were approaching networking incorrectly. They were asking people for information, advice and additional contacts as if it was a transaction. Networking is most effective when you see the opportunity to build a real connection or lasting relationship. Instead of engaging in conversation to get to know someone, people would often go right into what they needed, focusing on themselves and not the other person. That is not an effective way to build relationships and does not serve either party.

For example, I asked one client, "What did you learn about the person you just met?"

Confused, the client responded, "I don't think I asked her any questions about herself."

Imagine my frustration! I turned my focus from teaching *how to network* to *how to build relationships* particularly in a job search.

My goal was to make it simple for clients to understand. So, I put some structure around the stages of how relationships are developed. I came up with four simple words that capture the essence of building relationships. This four-word formula is also delightfully easy to remember: ***YOU, YOU, ME, YOU!***

There is one thing you need to remember when you meet someone new: **it is more about them** than it is about you!

We are constantly in situations where we meet new people, whether networking, joining a new group, or meeting our neighbors. You want to make a great first impression, don't you?

Unfortunately, you can easily sabotage that first impression by talking too much about yourself and not inquiring about the other person.

The good news? *YOU…YOU…ME…YOU* is a great tool to guide you in all conversations.

Let's walk through how *YOU, YOU, ME, YOU* is put into action.

After the initial firm handshake and name exchange, get the other person talking about themselves (YOU…YOU) by asking questions and showing interest. Try to keep this conversation going anywhere from 3-10 minutes.

After hearing about them, find an opportunity to share something about yourself (ME). For example, you too just got back from Florida and went to some of the same places, or share something about what you have done recently that might interest them based on what you heard about them. Hopefully, the other person gives you a chance to talk and listens. However, they might grab the conversation back to themselves and if they do, it is okay.

As you end the conversation, focus on the other person again (YOU) with a comment like. "It was nice to meet you and hear about your family!" Or hear about your travels, or hear about your work, or whatever. It can also be a simple "It has been a pleasure to meet you."

It is that simple. *YOU, YOU, ME, YOU.* In other words, the best strategy for making a great first impression is NOT by talking all about you, trying to impress with your stellar qualities and success. Instead make sure the other person walks away from the conversation:

★ feeling heard, valued and energized because you listened with interest

★ learning a nugget of something positive and memorable about you.

As Dale Carnegie said, "You can make more friends in two months by becoming interested in other people than you can in two years by trying to get other people interested in you!" (You will have that quote memorized by the end of this book!)

Notice in this *YOU, YOU, ME, YOU* formula, the conversation is about you only one-fourth of the time. It is three parts about them, one about you. Think of it as THEM, THEM, YOU, THEM.

It's easy! Be more interested in others. Make them feel great. That is how they will remember you. They will have a positive association of the time spent with you because you were truly interested in them.

These new interactions will create some real and lasting relationships, and all those people can be resources for you when you need something, be it a job, support, or the best mechanic in town.

When I introduced this concept to my clients, some were skeptical. Maybe you are too. Wipe the slate clean and give *YOU, YOU, ME, YOU* a try.

And yes, I realize there are all kinds of people in this world. Do you see yourself in one of these examples?

We all know people who talk too much.

Some people tend to talk too much about themselves. They may do it out of nervousness or a fear of awkward pauses in conversations. Some people just don't like the quiet. For others it's simply because they gain energy by talking and can't help themselves. For a few, it's an unhealthy ego and a belief they are one of the most interesting people in the world.

With that kind of talker, instead of the flow being *YOU, YOU, ME, YOU,* the conversation ends up being all (or mostly) about them. You don't want to be that person.

There are variations on being the one who talks too much. Here are a few examples:

ME, ME, ME, ME (not only do you look self-absorbed, you also bore other people to death)

YOU, ME, ME, ME (it becomes obvious that you're not that interested in them)

ME, ME, ME, YOU (the token display of interest at the end comes off as patronizing)

Relationships are a mutual exchange. You will find the most benefit if you stick with this simple formula as your guide:

- ❖ *YOU,*
- ❖ *YOU,*
- ❖ *ME,*
- ❖ *YOU.*

Talking too little can happen as well.

On the flip side of talking too much, some people tend to talk too little about themselves. For some it's nervousness or uncertainty around what to say about themselves. For others, the challenge is getting "airtime" among highly talkative people. The conversation ends up mostly with you contributing little to the conversation.

When this happens, the other person may walk away from the conversation feeling energized, yet they remember nothing about you or why a continued relationship might be beneficial (other than that you're a good listener). You need to make sure you get your ME inserted in the flow of conversation.

You do have something valuable to say and don't always need to be so polite and listen all the time. Take your turn and give them something memorable about you.

Avoid conversational ping pong.

If you're lucky and you're interacting with someone who also understands this strategy, you'll likely have a more balanced, give-and-take conversation that energizes and satisfies both of you. That said, don't assume conversations should be ME, YOU, ME, YOU.

Conversations rarely flow in such a rigid back-and-forth way. If you're waiting for the other person to reciprocate with a question every time you ask one, you'll likely set yourself up for frustration. True dialogue is not my turn, your turn, my turn, your turn.

It requires time, practice and reflection before *YOU, YOU, ME, YOU* takes on a natural flow. Remember that you are learning a new approach to building relationships and it is worth the time!

Specific ways to do this:

1. Ask three to four questions of the other person before talking about yourself.

2. Use positive body language to demonstrate you're interested in what others are saying.

3. Build your next question off what they have just said to keep them talking. This shows you're paying attention.

4. As you start to talk about yourself, use what you've learned about the other person to selectively emphasize things that you have in common.

5. As the conversation naturally reaches its end, ask one more question to bring the focus back to the other person. Look for opportunities to be helpful, whether it's providing information, advice, support, or just momentary companionship.

6. If it seems right, suggest meeting again to continue the conversation, and exchange contact information. Position your future meeting as an opportunity for mutual benefit.

The *YOU, YOU, ME, YOU* concept also applies to people we already know and know well. Even when you have a comfort level with a person, your conversations can be deeper and more meaningful when you employ this method.

When you are known as a good listener and caring person, you will be rewarded with wonderful relationships and plenty of resources and opportunities when the need arises. Relationships are developed by giving and receiving. The more you give to others, the more you receive back.

Some key things to remember:

➤ Avoid the trap of talking too much or too little, especially when you first meet someone.

➤ Ensure the other person walks away feeling heard and good about meeting you and would enjoy seeing you again.

➤ Show interest in others.

➤ Be curious. Ask more questions.

➢ Engage others with a simple statement: "That sounds so interesting, tell me more." Or use positive body language that encourages people to continue.

Relationship building does not have to be complicated. It can be as simple as YOU, YOU, ME, YOU! To help you relax and practice this concept, read on.

HELLO
I AM...

NETWORKING

CHAPTER FOUR

Networking

Networking. Just hearing the word gives many people a feeling of uneasiness. For some, networking does not feel genuine. For others who see it as asking for help, they may feel needy and very uncomfortable. And some people simply have a hard time talking to people they don't know!

However, a simple reframe can quell the nerves. Think of networking as making connections. We make connections, "aka networking," every day of our lives. Whether we are looking for a new doctor, hairdresser, or house realtor, we make connections for information, advice, and contacts.

One simple way to look at it is the definition I give my clients: *Networking is building and maintaining relationships for a mutual benefit to access and share information.* Read that last sentence again.

Networking is about relationships and sharing information. You can do that.

When you are networking, you are meeting with people you know and with people you do not know in order to provide that mutual benefit of information sharing. You have questions, others have answers. Others have questions, you have answers. Good networking, like a good relationship, is about reciprocity.

When I meet with new clients to provide guidance with their careers, I always get a sense of their comfort zone and experience around networking. I listen carefully to what networking means to them and how they do it. So many believe that networking is about "shortcutting," finding someone that works at a company where there is an opening or asking their contacts if anyone knows the hiring manager to send their resume. They don't see networking as building relationships with people who could potentially hire them in the future when an opening occurs.

The most successful job search strategy to find the right position is networking. Thus, you need to be able to network effectively (aka building relationships) *YOU, YOU, ME, YOU* is a great tool.

"You can make more friends in two months by becoming more interested in other people than you can in two years getting people interested in you." When I mention this Dale Carnegie quote encouraging someone to work on building the relationships first as part of networking, I often hear, "I don't have time for that; I need to find a job."

When someone has lost their job, sometimes they go into panic mode about needing to find a new job right away. However, chasing jobs in the advertised job market where there is so much competition is not always the best way to find that right fit. In many cases when hiring managers post a job, they already have a candidate in mind for the role due to networking.

Even if your resume makes it to the hiring manager via a contact, you have not built any kind of relationship and your resume still might be tossed or sent back to HR.

Helping job seekers understand the benefit of relationship building as part of their job search is very important. And of course, networking is not just for those needing a job. It's also the most successful way to meet future bosses, employees, colleagues, clients, referral partners and new friends. You also can be looking for referrals for hairdressers, great restaurants or best vacation spots. We always need others to help us, so none of us needs to be the Lone Ranger.

I've worked with a lot of folks who are sometimes hesitant to reach out to people they've lost contact with (i.e., a real relationship has not been sustained), and some are not comfortable meeting new people. Much of my work is helping clients understand and utilize the full and true power of relationship building and nurturing. If you are looking for a new position, networking helps you bypass the competition.

Networking is building relationships with reciprocity with people you know who can connect you to people they know for information, advice, and contacts—and when needed, access to the Hidden Job Market.

The Hidden Job Market represent jobs that are not published, positions that recently became open, or even roles that can be created because a company has a need for what you do. Positions have indeed been created for individuals who have the skills, talent, and personality that a company wants. The main way you access the Hidden Job Market is by building relationships with people.

The "silver bullet," the secret key, the golden ticket, whatever you want to call it, the primary ingredient to success is building relationships with people.

You want to be remembered. If you are job seeking, that means you don't just fire off a resume; it means you build and maintain relationships. How to do that? *YOU, YOU, ME, YOU.*

Relationships mean reciprocity, and reciprocity is about giving back to those who help you, even with a simple "Is there anything I can do for you?" Keith Ferrazzi, Author of *Never Eat Alone*, refers to relationships as showing generosity toward each other. When you come from a place of giving, others will appreciate your kind gestures. When the time comes for you to ask, I speculate others will be willing to help because you helped them first.

If someone has been generous with their time, you might send them a special thank you with a gift card from Starbucks or Dunkin Donuts with a note saying, "Have a cup of coffee on me."

Or, you could send a book or an article on a topic you discussed when you met. That would certainly leave a lasting impression.

Helping others understand the value of building relationship has become my mission. Many people need to be reminded that networking is really all about: developing *mutually beneficial relationships*. I often wonder "What would Dale Carnegie do?"

Before you read on, answer these three questions.

- Do you look forward to networking or dread it?
- What do you do when you meet someone new who you want to get to know better?
- What relationship building skill do you do well, and which one do you want to improve?

CHAPTER FIVE

Relationship Building

Whether you love meeting new people or dread it, you now can go forward with this simple tool: *YOU, YOU, ME, YOU.* Just remember that this tool is used to build RELATIONSHIPS and building trusting, reciprocal, long-lasting relationships takes time. The more you use this approach, the more natural and easier it becomes. You will find that you are no longer nervous about interacting!

A true relationship is not a transactional deal that involves buying or selling. A true relationship has an emotional component and desires to go beyond the transaction. It is relational, creating a connection and not just engaging in a transaction.

If the connection is positive, then people will remember you and even refer you to others.

However, if the interaction is negative, you may have lost not only one person, but many others because you will not be referred.

If the connection begins with a relational component, then you are more likely to have another interaction and a relationship as well. Of course, not all interactions or transactions need to turn into relationships. When you go to the grocery store, you are not going to develop a relationship with the cashier.

Or you might! There are times when unexpected relationships happen too. Several years ago, there was a boutique near my home that I went to frequently. Sometimes I bought things and other times I just liked to browse as the shop owner had great taste. One day, she asked my name, and from then on, she always greeted me by name with a friendly hello. I in turn asked her name. Every time I came to her store, we chatted a bit. On one of my frequent browsing trips, Barbara was extremely distracted and seemed to be upset. She apologized and said, "I'm sorry! I'm not myself. My husband just asked me for a divorce, and it took me by complete surprise."

I felt badly for her, but I also was glad she felt comfortable sharing her situation with me. We talked a bit and later that week, Barbara was still on my mind, so I sent her a handwritten note. I expressed that I was thinking of her during this difficult time and that I was praying for her too. The next time I went in she told me how much she appreciated my thoughtful gesture. I touched her heart, and when you touch someone's heart, they remember your kindness, and are reminded that kindness itself is alive and well. To this day, she remains a friend even attending one of my birthday celebrations.

Showing kindness to others is part of being human. We all need to remember how to relate on a human level to people in today's world.

You might find it easier to chat with a shop owner because you have nothing invested, no expectations. Yet when it comes to more formal networking that requires an introduction, you freeze up or feel unnatural. Don't despair. The *YOU, YOU, ME, YOU* concept is available for you anytime, anywhere. Relationship building can be a natural and easy process. Let it be!

Here are the Four Stages of Relationship Building.

Stage1 - *YOU*: Initiate

Stage 2 - *YOU*: Engage

Stage 3 - *ME*: Develop

Stage 4 - *YOU*: Strengthen

Stage 1: Initiate (YOU)

When you meet someone for the first time, extend your hand to greet them, use a firm handshake, confident eye contact, and repeat the person's name: "It is a pleasure to meet you, Sam!"

You might need to ask the person to repeat their name. You can do this with a simple, "I am sorry, I did not catch your name." By repeating the person's name right after an introduction, it will help you remember it and it makes the other person feel good too. As Dale Carnegie said, *"A person's name is the sweetest sound."*

If you have met the person before, or are not sure if you have, say their name but refrain from "nice to meet you." You can simply say, "It's good to see you here, Erica!"

Often when meeting new people, there isn't an opportunity to have a conversation beyond the initial greeting. Therefore, the first impressions may be the last one, so you want to make a good impression right from the start. Focus on putting the other person at ease. If there is an opportunity to have a conversation beyond the initial introduction, ask open-ended questions. Here are some conversation starters:

★ "What brought you to this event today?"

★ "Which speaker are you interested in hearing?"

★ "How do you know the host?"

Asking open-ended questions will show the other person that you are interested in learning more about them.

You may be tempted to start talking in this first stage because something will trigger a similar experience that you've had yourself that you will want to share. However, in this first phase of building a relationship, the focus is not on you.

In this stage, it is important to use your active listening skills: Use good eye contact, express words of acknowledgement to show you are listening, lean in as they talk, etc. Doing this will encourage the other person to keep talking. Don't worry, you will get your turn! In a few minutes, you can use what you hear in this first phase, so listen carefully. Stage 1, Initiate, is the first YOU.

Stage 2: Engage (YOU)

The second stage is to continue to build rapport with the other person. However, it is still not the time to share about you. Keep the conversation going with follow-up remarks and questions, such as: "Tell me more about that." "What was that like for you?" "That sounds so exciting." Try repeating their name when using comments that encourages the other person to speak.

If you cannot think of questions to continue to engage, your body language can also be a signal for someone to continue talking. Some people with a preference for introversion need time to process information; for them it can be challenging to ask or answer questions in the moment. Therefore, using positive body language like nodding your head, smiling, and keeping your body posture open with arms uncrossed and the palms of your hands open indicates you are interested in what they have to say.

During this second YOU stage, remember you want to learn more about the other person. It still is not time to share information about you. If you find yourself thinking of what you want to say, simply notice that. Instead of chiming in, you need to listen more. I know this can sometimes be hard to do.

For the most part, people like to share stories about themselves, especially if someone is encouraging them. Trust me, your patience will pay off in the end. Even if you don't get the opportunity in this interaction to talk about yourself, the other person will remember you. Why? Because you were more interested in hearing about them than you were in telling them about you!

In YOU, YOU, you want to go deeper with the other person. One of my best friends started a new business and when we met for breakfast, she told me about what she was doing. She talked for a few minutes and then said to me, "I want to hear what you are doing." Instead of talking about me, I responded, "Actually, I have not heard enough about your new business." She was delighted to share more, and my willingness to wait to talk about what I was doing further solidified our strong bond. Once you truly understand how to develop a lasting relationship, going through these stages will become second nature.

If you don't do Stage 2 well, the person will most likely feel the discussion was superficial and transactional.

Stage 3: Develop (ME)

In the third stage of the process, you can now start talking about yourself.

It might feel like a long time before you bring yourself into the conversation. It may be five minutes or even ten, which may be the longest time you have gone without talking. Side note, I read this section to my husband, Raphael, and he said, "If I had to wait five to ten minutes then I would forget what I was going to say."

You can imagine my comment to him, "Obviously you were not using your active listening skills!"

I kid my husband that he has given me great material for this book. If you find active listening a challenge, remember you are learning a new approach to building relationships. This requires you to change habits and behaviors. Your effort will absolutely be worth it.

When you pay attention to the other person before jumping in about yourself, (YOU, YOU, ME), it will be easier to segue into something about you that will feel more natural. As you move into this stage, acknowledge what you heard the person say and praise some of their key points, such as "You have had such an interesting career" or "You obviously love your family and are very proud of your children."

Everyone likes to hear a compliment, so even if you just met the person, don't hesitate to say something nice. As Dale Carnegie said, "Be hearty in approbation and lavish in praise."

Based on what you heard from the other person, share something of common interest or introduce something about yourself that you would want the other person to know. The Develop stage focuses on a two-way conversation, with a mutual exchange of information, asking questions and connecting the dots.

Notice I said that it is a *two-way* conversation. This is not about you finally getting to talk and taking over. This is about you initiating a connection with someone, engaging them in a real conversation, and developing rapport and common interest.

Stage 4: Strengthen (YOU)

The last stage is to strengthen the relationship between the two of you.

As you end the interaction, bring the conversation back to the other person. YOU, YOU, ME, YOU. When possible, shake their hand with the same firm shake and maintain good eye contact. For some people, a hug might be appropriate (I put this in for me because I am a hugger!). Pay attention to cultural and societal norms. For example, touching someone might be seen or perceived as disrespectful. Instead, mention how nice it was to talk to them: "I really enjoyed our conversation and hearing about (what you talked about)." Or you can simply say, "It was a pleasure meeting you (name) and I hope to see you at the next event."

If you feel that you made a nice connection and would like to get to know them better, ask if they would like to meet for coffee, lunch or drinks sometime soon. Remember, relationship building is not a transaction. It is an interaction between human beings that requires commitment, follow up, empathy, interest and authenticity. This doesn't have to be difficult! Sending a follow up note via mail, email or text would be a special touch.

The four stages of relationship building are as simple as:

1. Initiate = YOU
2. Engage = YOU
3. Develop = ME
4. Strengthen = YOU

You might not remember the words Initiate, Engage, Develop, Strengthen, but you will be able to remember *YOU, YOU, ME, YOU!*

All it takes is practice.

These four stages are not just for initial meetings with people. This process is about developing and maintaining relationships with everyone. Assume you are having lunch with a colleague, who tells you that her father has been in the hospital and her mother is worried. After she briefly tells you what happened, she turns to you and says, "Tell me what is going on with you and your project." Instead of talking about yourself, respond with "I can tell you about me later, I want to hear more about your parents. How is your father feeling now?" Let her continue to share what is going on, what is important to her right now.

The next time you see her, which could be in two weeks, two months or two years, you can start the conversation with "The last time you and I were together, you told me about your father. How is he doing?" Think of how she will feel because you remembered what is important to her. This is an example of creating an emotional bond between two people, maintaining a connection because you cared enough to listen and get to know the other person.

Here are some suggestions on how you can strengthen relationships.

- ❖ Write a handwritten note to say hello, thank you or get well. I send two to four handwritten notes each week because I am determined to keep this beautiful lost art alive.

- ❖ Send a card for a wedding anniversary or the anniversary of someone's death. One colleague's brother had died unexpectedly and she mentioned the two-year anniversary was approaching. I put a note on my calendar for the day to remind me to send her a note letting her know I was thinking of her.

- ❖ Send a text or make a quick call to a friend whose family member is sick, asking how they are feeling and that you are thinking of them.

❖ Pick up a small gift just because you know someone will like it.

❖ Pick up the tab for breakfast, lunch, dinner or even a cup of coffee.

❖ Send a birthday card, a note through LinkedIn wishing them a Happy Birthday, or for more personal relationships through Facebook. You might have discovered their birth date during the Develop stage or noticed it on a social media site. In my circle of friends, I am known for remembering friends and family members' birthdays. I often call to sing to them. In return many sing to me on my day (payback time). Remembering someone's birthday is such a wonderful way to develop a deeper bond with them. Birthdays are the anniversary of the day you were born into this world. What a world it is with you in it. I love birthdays!

Each kind gesture is another knot to strengthen the relationship. Mark special events in your calendar. Every day I look at my calendar to see whom I want to remember. I send a card, a handwritten note or a short "thinking of you" text.

Maybe there is a relationship in your life that you want to strengthen, or someone you've lost touch with over the years. Think about the four stages and give yourself an honest review. Do you Initiate? Engage? Develop? Strengthen? Is there anything lacking in each stage that you can begin to enhance or that you realize you are not doing at all?

You will realize with just a little bit of effort, that you can improve your relationship building skills. Not everyone you meet is going to become your best friend. Nevertheless, using *YOU, YOU, ME, YOU* will certainly help you build a richer and stronger bond.

I love the story of the relationship between Thomas Jefferson and John Adams. They had a strong, mutual, respectful and admirable bond. Even though they did not share the same political views, they enjoyed each other's company (most of the time) and were able to maintain a relationship. Throughout their lives, they wrote letters to each other to stay connected, sharing their thoughts and opinions about the emerging country and what was going on within their families. Their correspondence kept their bond strong until the day they died, both on the same date, July 4, 1826, the 50th anniversary of the Declaration of Independence.

You may not go down in history like these two men. However, you certainly can be remembered as someone who valued people and created meaningful relationships. It truly is as simple as *YOU, YOU, ME, YOU.*

CHAPTER SIX

Everyday Situations

The *YOU, YOU, ME, YOU* model is a great tool to help you speak with someone, network, and build relationships. Once you implement this concept, you will notice how helpful and valuable it is!

Every day we encounter situations that challenge our relationship skills. This is where we need to make some adjustments. How we react to one another can create either a positive or negative experience. Here are some situations you might encounter.

More than likely, you know a **Self-Absorbed Sarah** who, when you first met, talked all about herself and never asked anything about you. We all know people who never ask about us because they are too wrapped up talking about their own lives. When you attempt to speak, Sarah steers the conversation back to herself. You tell yourself that perhaps the next time will be different, and for once, Sarah will ask "What is going on with you." However, what are the odds that will happen? I wouldn't expect it.

It is easy to speculate why some people come across as self-absorbed, telling only their tales, unaware that others have stories to share too. Maybe it's an insecurity or inflated ego. Maybe they don't know what questions to ask or they become nervous in conversations. Whatever the reason, they need this book for the tool YOU, YOU, ME, YOU!

Unless you tell Sarah, she will continue to talk all about herself. Because you have not mentioned how this bothers you, she may assume you are interested in her stories and will continue talking and talking, barely coming up for air.

The same goes for **Hijack Harry.** You've started to tell Harry about an experience you've had and suddenly, Harry jumps in and takes over, going on and on about what happened to him. When this happens, you are no longer the "speaker," but now the "captive listener" to someone else's story.

Likely, Self-Absorbed Sarah and Hijack Harry don't realize that they have monopolized the conversation. It would not occur to them to say, "Enough about me, tell me something about you. What is going on in your life?" Ironically, if they were to throw the conversation back, you may be caught off guard and respond, "Oh, not much." Only later do you realize you could have shared some wonderful things that are going on in your own life.

Now, armed with information in this book, you can tactfully move the conversation to a better balance of sharing. *YOU, YOU, ME, YOU* is a skill that can be developed.

Some people are comfortable in new situations because they are curious by nature and love to hear about other people. Asking questions and developing relationships comes easily to them. You too may be curious but might not feel as comfortable engaging in conversation. That is where *YOU, YOU, ME, YOU* is your trusty guide.

Remember that *YOU, YOU, ME, YOU* is flexible. Perhaps you know a shy person or someone who is more introverted, and they prefer to be less focused on themselves. Maybe they don't particularly like being the center of attention because all eyes are on them. Or for whatever reason, they let the other person do most of the talking. They might not say anything about themselves, unless you ask.

When you meet a **Shy Sally**, remember the four stages of *YOU, YOU, ME, YOU*, but honor their comfort level. Most people do like to talk about themselves, however, this is not the case with ALL people.

"Hi, Sally, my name is Oscar Outgoing, Great to meet you."

Sally: "Hello."

Oscar: "Have you been coming to this networking group for a while?"

Sally: "Yes."

Sally says nothing more.

Oscar nods. "I think we have a mutual friend, Lauren Johnson!"

Sally replies: "Oh."

That's it. That's all Sally says.

So, Oscar continues, "Lauren is a colleague of mine, I didn't realize she lived in this town."

Sally: "Yes she does."

Oscar: "Lauren speaks so highly of you. How did the two of you meet?"

Notice, the question is not about Shy Sally, but her relationship with her friend. Sometimes, you might need to talk more about your mutual connection before someone is comfortable talking about themselves.

Oscar can guide the conversation to where Sally feels more comfortable, more at ease. When Sally feels more at ease, you can move to asking questions about her and what she does. You can still initiate and engage even if the other person does not want to talk about themselves. If you can find some common rapport, you will get to know them a little bit in a roundabout way. Your willingness to be patient and kind will make a positive impression on the people you meet.

You can adapt the *YOU, YOU, ME, YOU* skill as needed. For example, a humble person may not necessarily be shy, but **Humble Hannah** will want to talk more about *you* than herself. She may be uncomfortable sharing the spotlight. So, she usually downplays what she does. Not everyone wants to let others know about what they do. Their modesty holds them back. Talking about common interests can draw them out.

What about the person who has a low opinion of themselves? They have a hard time talking about what is going in their lives. As part of my work as a Career Consultant, I help people develop more confidence in themselves and in their ability to achieve success. When a person has more confidence, they are more at ease talking with others and sharing what they have to offer.

Occasionally we may encounter a **Needy Ned** who from time to time is looking for advice, support and empathy. From Ned's end, it is all ME, ME, ME, ME. There are times in life when you may choose to give all your focus to the other person. This person has something going on and needs to talk, to process. They need empathy and to be heard. This isn't the time for you to expect to be asked, "So how are you doing?"

This also is not the time for you to hijack the conversation and say, "*I know just how you feel because I experienced the same thing.*" You may have experienced a similar situation; however, your reaction and feelings are yours. Do you really know how the other person feels? Are you in their mind and body? How you felt does not mean the other person feels the same way.

The Needy Ned in your life at that moment needs you to listen with your heart and empathetic ear. Ask, "Is there something specific that I can do for you that will help you through this difficult time?" Think of what you would want from your friend if the tables were turned.

Another time to adapt the formula of *YOU, YOU, ME, YOU* is when someone is grieving. The death of a loved one is all about YOU, YOU YOU, YOU. When **Grieving Grace** is dealing with the death of her loved one, she does not want to hear how you dealt with a similar loss. During this difficult time, Grace needs someone to listen to her with empathy. You can say, "I am so sorry for your loss. My heart goes out to you during this very sad time." Or if you are religious, simply say, "I will hold you and your loved ones in my prayers." Saying less is the best response.

Some of our everyday conversations can be difficult ones as with Grieving Grace. It could also be with a close family member, friend or someone you just met who is the dominator and wants to control the conversation. Within minutes of your talking about something that happened to you, **Donnie Dominator,** like Harry Hijacker, jumps in with "I've been there and…." or "that happened to me and…."

At this point you are hearing all about them, and they are not hearing anything about you.

Sometimes the conversation will wander back to you. Sometimes you can gracefully retrieve it by saying, "Let me finish telling about what happened to me." The best scenario would be Donnie Dominator realizes what he did and might even say, "I am sorry, finish what you started to tell me."

Let's say he just keeps talking. Do you *want* to share your story? You can certainly say, "Let me finish telling you about…." However, do you think he cares? Would he really be interested in what you have to say? Do you even want to bother? This is your call.

The idea of *YOU, YOU, ME, YOU* is to help you navigate conversations and show you are interested in building a relationship. This idea is a mutual sharing, and a benefit to both of you. You will find that you can make a good lasting impression by being tolerant and respectful of the other person, even if you do not end up with a truly mutual relationship.

Another type of listener is the limited listener, **Distracted Diane.** She does not maintain eye contact; she looks beyond your head to see who is near. Diane is more concerned about what she might be missing than listening to you.

Distracted Diane will ask about you to be polite while also scoping out the room. She is listening to everyone around you; her focus is not on you. What can you do? First, you don't have to be rude and abruptly walk away. You can end the chat with a firm handshake, good eye contact, and a "It was nice meeting you Diane." Then you can initiate another conversation with someone who is interested in the mutual benefit of conversation and information sharing. Their focus is on getting to know you better.

It is okay to extract yourself from any conversation that is with a ME, ME, ME, ME person. Use some diplomacy, and say, "Excuse me, but I need to get a drink/go to the ladies' room/get to an appointment/catch a train to get home/or connect with my colleague who just arrived."

When you get caught in a one-way discussion, use direct and polite language to stop the conversation: "I hate to interrupt you, but I need to go to_____." The other person may be totally unaware of their impact on others. They will not be offended with your abrupt exit, so do not feel you are being rude.

What about the "phubber"? When I first heard this word, I did not know what it meant. Phubbing means to ignore one's companion in order to pay attention to phones or other mobile devices. "Phone snubbing" is phubbing. I am not going to ask if this has happened to you. I bet it has. The question is: Are you guilty?

The phubber is like the **Limited Listener**, preoccupied with their phone and only half listening to what you have to say. Perhaps one way to get their attention would be to send them a text: "Can you put down your cell phone and talk to me?" Seriously, just exit gracefully.

Nothing in life is perfect, and the road to building real relationships has some twists and turns. The formula of *YOU, YOU, ME, YOU* will help you navigate the path and help you steer clear of those who are not in it for mutual benefit.

I hope you have gained many tips from this chapter. Maybe you can identify with one of the characters and make some adjustments to how you interact with others.

CHAPTER SEVEN

Sticky Situations

We encounter **sticky situation**s every day that we need to learn how to best maneuver our way around others. It doesn't have to be difficult if you know what to say and when. The main objective is to avoid offending or hurting anyone's feelings.

For example, dealing with a pushy salesperson can sometimes be challenging. Not every salesperson understands this concept of *YOU, YOU, ME, YOU*. **Pushy Pete** who wants your business can certainly make a one-time sale. However, Pete will miss out on repeat business because he does not take the time to develop the relationship first.

Build a solid relationship with your new customer and reap the benefits for a long time. The customer is the priority, and the sale is the second. The *YOU, YOU, ME, YOU* concept can change your career and bottom line.

There was a sticky situation I encountered with a salesperson, Max, who tried to convince me to use his company to design a website for an organization I founded http://www.careerengage-boston.com. We provide career advice for early- to mid-career professionals via coaching, webinars, and seminars. In my initial phone call with Max, I felt he was more transactional than relational. He talked a lot about himself and what he could do for me, yet he asked little about what I needed.

Sadly, Max did not play by the *YOU, YOU, ME, YOU* game book. But I liked his services, and his timing to reach out to me was perfect. We set up another time to talk because I wanted to give him a second chance. I'm glad I did! This time Max talked about wanting to make sure I was comfortable with the product. If I needed more time to decide, that was not a problem. He was willing to make a deal on a second website. This time Max put his attention on me and my needs. He listened, and I felt heard. Max wanted to enter into a business relationship and not just a one-time transaction.

There are many instances in life that asking questions can turn out to be awkward and uncomfortable especially with people you just met. Asking if someone has children can be a sensitive topic. If you do ask about children, and the person replies no, really listen to what they say. Did they answer abruptly? Did they provide a reason why they don't have children? *YOU, YOU, ME, YOU* is about keeping your attention on the other person and getting to know them. Your goal is to have the other person feel at ease.

I get asked all the time, "Do you have children?"

My response is "No, I don't; however, I do have nieces and nephews who are an important part of my life." In my late 20s, I decided not to have children. It was a personal decision and one I never regretted. However, there are women who are unable to have children who desperately wanted them. Therefore, talking about what your children are doing or assuming that the other person has a family is not always a good ice breaker.

There are many other ways to engage in conversation. You can ask:

- Do you live or grow up in the area?
- Do you have siblings, and do they live in the area?
- If you are an invited guest to someone's home, you could ask "How do you know the host and hostess?"

Let's move onto an aspect of relationship building that can be used when you are not sure how to move away from an uncomfortable situation. One of my favorite quotes by St. Francis of Assisi, Founder of the Franciscan Order, "for it is in giving that we receive" says it all. It is about giving without any expectation of receiving in return. There could be someone in your life where you are always giving and feeling the relationship is one-sided. Taking the time to do something nice for people will come back to you unequivocally. My father used to say, "There are givers and takers in this world. You decide who you want to be."

I was very fortunate to have parents who were givers and always thinking of others. My parents were very involved in our community. My twin sister Johanna and I were given a scholarship to a Catholic School in Junior High because of my mother's volunteer work with the school. You can imagine what a blessing this was to a family with six children.

Small gestures go a long way.

Small things add up.

You cannot predict the gifts, tangible and intangible, that will emerge when you focus your attention on caring about other people. Even in sticky situations that are uncomfortable, you can turn it into a positive situation. Being thoughtful, taking the time for people, and using genuine words and behaviors will draw people to you. Dale Carnegie believed in letting the other person save face by using tact and being considerate of their feelings.

Now more than ever, for our society and world, we want to keep alive that human touch and pay attention to what is important... our relationships!

Building relationships is not solely for business reasons. Perhaps, your goal is more personal, for example, looking for a date.

Another sticky situation can be on a date. My husband and I were out to dinner one evening, and our table was so close to the one next to us that I could hear their conversation. They appeared to be a couple on a first date. (Honestly, I was not eavesdropping). What caught my attention was that I only heard the man talk, not ever the woman. It wasn't a conversation at all. He talked. And talked. And talked. He did not ask her anything. I observed her listening politely and wondered what was going on in her mind. I certainly was thinking, "Is he ever going to ask anything about her and what she does?"

If I were coaching this woman, I would recommend her to interject something about herself. It can be something triggered by what the date said: "When you mentioned about _____, I had a similar experience with _____." What a difference it would make if the man realized he was talking too much and said, "I've talked enough about myself; I want to hear more about you." Switching the focus from ME to YOU could make the difference between a first date and any chance of a second.

Dating in today's world of high digital and app use, it is challenging finding a compatible partner. In the early stages, dating relies less on chemistry and more on checking the boxes or filling out an online profile with your criteria for the perfect match. Your first interaction, or even date, might be text or video chat.

In Chapter 4, when we talked about networking, we focused on building relationships with people you know who can introduce you to people they know for information, advice and contacts. For job seekers, networking can provide access to the Hidden Job Market.

What about using the concept of YOU, YOU, ME, YOU to access that compatible person you are seeking in your personal life? I call it the *Hidden Compatible Market.* In this market, you ask for information, advice and contacts so you can meet as many people as you can to find that compatible match. Just as a job needs to be the right fit, the same applies to a partner.

So, where do you start? The first step is to identify your criteria for the compatible person. For example,

★ Identify the characteristics, qualities and interests you are hoping to find in another person.

★ Brainstorm with a friend places you would more than likely find this type of person.

★ Develop a few conversational questions that will help you determine if the person you meet is truly compatible with you.

This approach is not for everyone. However, if you apply this model you will build relationships with people who can refer you and perhaps play matchmaker.

Now, let's say through your contacts you found someone you are willing to meet. Just like a job interview, a first date (at any age!) can cause you to be nervous. The good news, you will be more at ease now because you have the four-stage *YOU, YOU, ME, YOU* as your guide.

Picture the first date. Both people need to learn enough about each other to determine if there is going to be a Date #2. What happens on a first date? Who is it really all about? Is it *YOU, YOU, ME, YOU* or is it ME, ME, YOU, ME? To be honest, it depends. You both need ample time to share so you can determine if there is enough common interest to continue.

No matter the situation, use your relationship building skills to find information, advice and contacts for all kinds of needs. The *YOU, YOU, ME, YOU* concept is adaptable and at your service.

CHAPTER EIGHT

Social Media and the Digital Age

Social media postings of graduations, birthdays, showers, weddings, and pregnancies from the announcement to the baby bump to the birth (that often includes videos) allow us to stay current in each other's lives. We also learn about people who passed away and funeral arrangements. We share condolences. If we use social media wisely, it is wonderful!

Platforms like Facebook and LinkedIn were developed to build, maintain and strengthen personal and professional relationships. Were these platforms intended to replace human interaction? No. Think about it. Albert Mehrabian, Professor Emeritus of Psychology, UCLA, developed a Communication Model of what we pay most attention to when we communicate with one another. His findings are: the use of one's voice such as tone, intonation and volume represent 38%, the literal meaning of our words represent 7% and 55% of our body language in how we communicate. However, with social media, we lose tone and body language cues. Therefore, we need to choose our words carefully to avoid misunderstanding. Have you ever read a post where you thought the person responded inappropriately? Perhaps if you were able to read their body language you might have interpreted it differently.

One social media platform for professional use is LinkedIn as opposed to Facebook, which is more personal in nature. LinkedIn is used by those who own a business, individuals looking for a job, or people to fill jobs, promoting a book (that would be me) or finding new connections. LinkedIn is your virtual network! Therefore, maintaining relationships with your existing connections and building new ones with the right people can open exciting new opportunities. Having a positive and professional online presence is an important aspect of career success.

For example, I used LinkedIn to initiate a relationship with someone I wanted as a first-degree connection in my network. He was the President of Dale Carnegie Inc. You might say I was kind of a "stalker," but a nice one.

Using many of the principles of Dale Carnegie, I started to follow, like, comment and share many of his postings with my network. LinkedIn notified him of my activity and when the timing was right, I asked the President to be a first-degree connection. I was thrilled when he accepted! I continued to acknowledge and share his posts developing a virtual relationship. Before long, he replied to one of my comments using my name. It made my day!

Remember to use *YOU, YOU, ME, YOU* concept and understand that developing virtual relationships will take more time. It will be worth your effort!

We can probably *all* agree that technology has made a great impact on *all* generations. There is much to appreciate. However, as we move forward with ever-evolving technology, it is important not to lose sight of what has kept us connected in the past.

Have you ever thought about what life would be like without cell phones, texting, Facebook, Twitter and all things digital? When I was younger, if you wanted to talk to someone, you picked up the phone. If you wanted directions, you looked at a map or asked someone and if you thanked someone for giving you a gift, you sent a note in the mail.

"When I was younger" is a phrase often heard from older generations to the next. We like to reminisce about what *we* did growing up. We sometimes believe that our times were the best ones.

Perhaps previous generations felt more connected, because of face-to-face interaction and conversation. One of the reasons I wrote this book was that I became acutely aware people were not having actual conversations. While they were on their cell phones, they were also engaging with others. I started to ask millennials why they used their technology to communicate instead of having face-to-face conversations. Their responses? "I don't know what to say. I don't know how to engage in a conversation, and it is much easier and quicker to send a text."

Also disappearing from today's world is the art of sending a handwritten note. Such a note could acknowledge a kind gesture, a simple "thinking of you," or sympathy for the loss of a loved one.

So much of our history, particularly expressing love for one another, was documented through handwritten notes (in cursive another dying art!) Remember how Thomas Jefferson and John Adams strengthened their relationship through writing to each other.

My husband Raphael strengthened our relationship by leaving a handwritten note on my pillow each time he left on a business trip. Those beautiful notes I read before I went to sleep captured how much we loved each other. I still cherish them.

Handwritten notes are a way I stay connected with my friends, family and colleagues. I rarely miss special occasions such as birthdays or anniversaries. I recently sent a note to my neighbor after catching up over coffee. I told her know how great it was to spend time together and hear what she was doing. She called to thank me for the card. We made another coffee date. Scheduling another date for coffee weeks or months away helps you sustain the relationship you have already developed.

Using social media to enhance your connections is wonderful. Many relationships have been developed using technology. However, I believe too many people of all ages spend too much time on their cell phones, Facebook and other forms of social media.

This practice does not belong solely to the younger generations. How many times do you see mid-to-older adults who cannot put their phones down? I've observed many families where the parents are constantly checking their cell phones while the kids are taking selfies or playing games on their devices. They barely look at one another. Many times, I have been tempted to say something like, "You are missing a wonderful opportunity to have a conversation with each other! Learn about their day! Share stories about yours!" But of course, I don't and yet it deeply saddens me.

Be honest—are you one of these people?

Try this: When you are with your family, significant other or friends having dinner or a night at home, have a "no cell" time. Without the distraction, you will pay more attention to the person speaking. Maybe you will learn something that pleasantly surprises you.

In this "no cell" scenario, you can use the *YOU, YOU, ME, YOU* approach effectively to cultivate a great conversation and build the relationship.

Another suggestion, when you are having a meal with family, friends or colleagues, share the concept about *YOU, YOU, ME, YOU*. When someone starts talking too soon about themselves, remind them the goal is to listen more than you speak. Say it with a smile, of course!

Have fun with it! See how long someone can go without talking about themselves. Ask each other questions to see how long you can keep the other person talking.

Really listen to each other in conversations. Imagine what you could learn. Imagine how you will feel by being genuinely interested in what the other person has to say.

To help you build, maintain, and strengthen online relationships, especially using Facebook and LinkedIn here are some key highlights to remember:

➢ Avoid the trap of talking too much about what you are doing.

➢ Show interest in others' posts and comment on their activity.

➢ If you sense someone is going through a hard time, pick up the phone or send them a message offline to show you care.

➢ Avoid "liking" everything. It is easy to do and can come across as "checking the box" and not caring enough about the relationship to comment. One of the benefits of LinkedIn is to be "found" by others, especially if you are looking for a job. Commenting and sharing on post and articles will give you great visibility with your connections. It is also a way to sustain relationships with those you don't often see.

➢ If you haven't seen someone face-to-face in a while, ask that person for coffee or dinner. If that doesn't work, schedule a "lunch time chat" or "virtual coffee time." If possible, use the latest software for online meetings, chat and mobile collaboration.

➢ Be curious. Ask questions. Even a simple "that sounds so interesting, tell me more" can keep the conversation going.

> Let's not forget Dale Carnegie's book "*How to Win Friends and Influence People in the Digital Age*" where you can learn more about bringing his practices and techniques online.

Jayne Mattson is not the first to write about how social media has affected our lives. I certainly will not be the last, yet the challenge remains: How do we keep the human interaction alive while technology, social media, and digital enhancements continue to advance.

We can't rely upon Facebook, Instagram, Snapchat, Twitter, LinkedIn and other social media

platforms to become our main source of staying connected. However, we can use social media to create awareness and education. We can talk to our friends, family, followers and connections about the benefits of meaningful personal and business relationships.

Are you up for the challenge to pay closer attention to your online presence and actions? After all, that's important for your relationships too.

Are you willing to move from your self-interest to the interest of others? When using social media, remember the four simple words that capture the essence of building relationships everywhere: *YOU, YOU, ME, YOU.* When you connect with someone, in person or on social media, it is more about them than it is about you.

Social media and digital communication will continue to advance, getting more sophisticated as technology evolves. However, the lack of solid effective interpersonal skills in the workplace and in our personal lives will trigger the need to have more balance. Our innate need as humans is to feel valued, loved and wanted. The best way to show this is through our face-to-face interactions. And to keep going with *YOU, YOU, ME, YOU.*

Social media and the digital world are here to stay. Social media has transformed how we live our lives. I feel strongly that we need to pick up the phone more and talk to one another whether for an invitation to an event, resolving an issue or just to say "hello."

So, let's embrace the new and maintain some of the "old."

CHAPTER NINE

Parting Thoughts

While driving home from dinner one evening when my nieces were very young, I heard the rustling of papers in the backseat. As I turned to see what it was, they each had a sheet of paper with a list of 20 questions. "Okay, Auntie, it is our time for us to ask *you* questions!"

I was so excited! One by one, they took turns asking me questions. That day it was about *ME, ME, ME, and ME.* I was in heaven! To this day, that drive home is one of my favorite memories with them.

Ever since they were young, I encouraged a "No Cell Zone" when we were together. I wanted them to feel comfortable interacting with others face-to-face, asking questions and learning about one another's lives without relying upon technology.

In these moments, I feel the legacy of my father living through me, hearing his words, "Honey, Honey, Honey if you read this book (*How to Win Friends and Influence People*), you will always be successful."

Earlier on, we talked about networking, which is simply about building relationships with people you know who can connect you to people they know. We discussed the four stages:

- ❖ *Initiate* connection, reach out to shake someone's hand, share eye contact and a smile, repeat the person's name with the introduction (YOU).

- ❖ *Engage* more deeply, develop rapport by asking questions about the other person (YOU).

- ❖ *Develop* the relationship, start to share something about you, ideally bringing in something you heard about the other person (ME).

- ❖ *Strengthen* what you have started to develop into a lasting relationship (YOU).

Millions of people today are connected to tablets, smartphones and computers. We sometimes seem more connected to our devices than people.

Yet, you are here reading this book. You are part of the solution in keeping our human interactions alive in this age of digital evolution. I thank you for your contribution!

So, where do we go from here? Let me recommend some ideas to move from technology to the human connection.

1. *Unplug:* Designate one day each month (or more!) as a day when you unplug from your devices. See what effect this has on you. You may be surprised that you will feel good as opposed to feeling stressed worrying that you've missed out on something because you were offline. Who knows? You may even choose to go unplugged one day per week!

2. *No Cell Zone Time*: Choose times each day to put the phones away. Maybe it's breakfast or dinner (or both!). Use mealtime to have conversations or just be with yourself.

3. *Face-to-face* (F2F) *Day:* Ask a friend, family member or colleague you typically stay in touch with via text, social media or email to meet you in person for coffee, lunch or dinner. Tell them what you are doing and

encourage them to have a F2F day with someone they know. Start a ripple effect.

4. *Virtual Coffee Chats*: Before you accept a LinkedIn connection, look at the person's profile who wants to connect with you. Many people do not give a reason why they want to be a connection. Don't just click and accept every invitation. If you are interested in learning more about them, ask for a "virtual morning coffee chat." Choose to have a relationship with your online connections. Since you can't meet them in person, a phone conversation is the next best thing to get to know them better.

5. *Handwritten notes:* Take the time to send 1 or 2 handwritten notes each week to a friend or family member.

These are just a few simple ways to get started. You might have some of your own ideas. Share them with others. You can also share them with me at Jayne@JayneMattson.com.

The *YOU, YOU, ME, YOU* concept is simple. And it works. Whether you are networking, conversing in everyday situations, dealing with sticky situations, or navigating social media and technology, you can apply the *YOU, YOU, ME, YOU* concept.

We can all make a difference in what we want our future to look like for ourselves, our families and future generations. How? By continuing to talk with each other through meaningful conversations.

Ever since I can remember I've wanted to leave a legacy. It needs to be more than "Jayne was a wonderful person." I want to be remembered for making a greater impact on people's lives. I am hopeful that YOU, YOU, ME, YOU will be part of that legacy.

My wish is that you are inspired to work harder on your face-to-face interactions to strengthen your good relationships, repair damaged relationships, and develop new ones.

After all, as human beings we are meant to be connected socially and physically.

This small book has a huge mission. We can truly see each other, hear each other, help each other. We can have real relationships that benefits all parties.

If you ever have any doubt that you can develop meaningful and lasting relationships, hear the words of my father for you, "Honey, honey, honey, of course you can do it!" Cultivating and nurturing good relationships doesn't need to be complicated. Just remember these four simple words and your life will be enriched.

It is all about ***YOU, YOU, ME, YOU!***

Acknowledgements

Without the help of family, friends and colleagues, this book would not have been published. First, I want to thank my kindred spirit, Debbie Gillespie Grecco. She has encouraged me for so many years to write a book. I feel so blessed to have a dear friend who gives me unconditional love and support for whatever I do. The other person who never stops encouraging me is my husband Raphael. Writing a book takes time away from family and friends. He always understood when I needed to work on the book being patient and loving along the way.

I want to thank my initial readers, Cheri Paulson, Ed Evarts and Trisha Griffin-Carty who gave me preliminary feedback that helped pave the way toward future revisions. Louisa Mattson (no relation) proofread the book for grammar and punctuation. Since I have many quotations and conversations in the book, her feedback was invaluable that will benefit the reader. My sister Janis Callan's feedback was also important. Anytime you write about your family, you want to know they approve and that you get it right. Thank you to Rob Mattson (is related) for reading the book giving him only a day to read it. His precise comments lead me to the finish line.

I saved the best for last! I could not possibly have published this book without the guidance, patience and wordsmithing from my dear friend and colleague Trisha Griffin-Carty. We read each sentence in every chapter 2-3 times to make sure I was able to capture the essence of each character and every stage of *You, You, Me, You*. I feel incredibly blessed to have someone in my life that wants as much success for me as I want for myself.

About the Author

An authentic relationship builder and Career Management Consultant, Jayne Mattson is known for cultivating confidence in her clients, allowing them to explore new career options through relationship building and practical job search techniques. A skilled facilitator and inspirational speaker, Jayne speaks frequently on topics that include "Building Confidence as a Foundation of Career Success" and "How to Create Virtual Relationships Using LinkedIn."

She authors and contributes to articles on numerous career topics that have appeared in *The New York Times*, CareerBuilder, Monster, CIO.com and Mashable.com.

Jayne is an avid racewalker, who loves to travel, especially to France. She lives in the Boston area with her husband Raphael and two cats Leo and Lily.

If you are interested in having Jayne help you manage your career or to speak to your organization, reach out to her at: www.jaynemattson.com or at Jayne@jaynemattson.com.